MUSIC BUSINESS RESOURCE MANUAL

Lots of Helpful Information

and Resources for

Independent Musicians

Judy Caplan Ginsburgh

Music Business Resource Manual

Copyright © 2014 Judy Caplan Ginsburgh

All rights reserved.

ISBN: 1-885711-30-1
ISBN: 978-1-885711-30-4

DEDICATION

This Manual is dedicated to all musicians out there who have questions about the business side of making music. As a seasoned performer and touring and recording artist, I wish to share some of the things I have learned along the way. When you are an independent musician, you have to wear many hats. We all love to create and perform. But, it is much more difficult to take care of the more "boring" aspects of our profession – like booking, taxes, contracts, etc. It is my hope to share some of the things that worked for me and helped me "keep it all together" in order to enjoy and make a living as a musician.

CONTENTS

	Background	1
1	Ten Easy Things	3
2	Who Are You?	4
3	Letting Others Know About You	6
4	Creating A Press Kit	7
5	Developing a Website	9
6	Marketing Options	11
7	Making A CD	12
8	Recording and Producing Your CD	15
9	Selling and Marketing Your Recording	16
10	UPC/ISBN Bar Coding For Products	18
11	Copyright Information	19
12	Performance Rights and Mechanical Rights	23
13	Performing	24
14	Tips for Managing Yourself	26
15	Diversify: Thinking Outside of The Music Box	27
16	Tax Tips	29
17	Resources	32

SOME BACKGROUND

I first sang on stage when I was 6 years old. This is probably when my parents realized that I had been blessed with a rare gift...a crystal clear voice with almost a 4-octave range. As a child, I participated in many Community Musical Theatre productions. When I was about 9 years old, I was chosen to sing in a children's chorus with the local symphony orchestra. When I attended high school, I was in the Concert Choir and Swing Choir and had the opportunity to participate in festivals, All State and Honor Choirs. I got a guitar at age 13 and taught myself to play with a Mel Bay chord book and by listening to recordings of folk music (mainly Joan Baez, Judy Collins, Joni Mitchell, James Taylor, Leonard Cohen, etc.). Then I was exposed to camp music and specifically Jewish camp music. I was hooked. I became a song leader for our Jewish youth movement and I continued to participate in musical theatre and even some opera. For college, I was accepted into the prestigious Indiana University Jacobs School of Music where I received a Bachelor of Music degree in Vocal Performance with a minor in Theatre.

When I married and moved to the Washington, DC area, I began singing in synagogues as a cantorial soloist. I also became a music specialist at several preschools. Soon I had produced my first recording (a record – a round, black disc made of vinyl. Ancient!) with a goal to sell 1000 copies in 10 years. I never would have believed I would sell all 1000 copies in less than 6 months!

And so, a career was born. Soon I produced 2 more recordings. In 1997, my husband and I moved to Louisiana, my home. I found myself traveling all over North America presenting concerts, leading teacher in-service training sessions and producing more recordings.

For approximately ten years, I ran a company that I founded called Jewish Entertainment Resources. It was created to try to unify the community of contemporary Jewish performers, to help them network, and to provide them with information and resources to learn more about the business side of music and further their careers.

Throughout my thirty-year career, I have learned a great deal about the music business. I have won numerous awards for my recordings and my work and I have accomplished so much more than I ever dreamed possible. In this publication, I want to share some of the wisdom I have gained through the years.

As each year goes by, being a musician becomes more and more a business. It is more difficult to compete, it is more difficult to stay ahead and we must forever find time to "do our homework." I hope these resources will help you, the performer, to be able to learn more about the **business** of being a performer. I also hope you will use me as a resource. You can reach me by email at **judy@judymusic.com** or by phone at (318) 442-8863.

TEN EASY THINGS YOU CAN DO TO FURTHER YOUR MUSICAL CAREER

1) Start a mailing list (fan list, data base, etc.) Invest in some data base software and begin entering information into this list on your computer. Log in all people who write to you about your music, all people who purchase your music, people who attend your shows, names from any mailing list you can find, etc.

2) Attend a Business Conference, seminar or webinar to learn more about the business side of your career. Sometimes Arts Councils and Community Foundations offer workshops on financial topics, grant writing, marketing, etc. Check it out.

3) Read everything you can find that will give you more information about the business side of music, touring, marketing, etc. Subscribe to on-line e-zines, and trade magazines. (See resource section of this book)

4) Listen to what others are doing. Network with them. Share. Ask for their opinions.

5) Video some of your own concerts and watch by yourself or with others you trust and critique your performance. What was good? What did not work? What could be better? Look at the whole package, not just the music. (speaking, dress, body language, etc.)

6) Go to one retreat, gathering, or conference just for you. Find something where there is no pressure to perform. Somewhere where you can relax, learn and be inspired to look at things with fresh eyes and hear things with fresh ears.

7) If you have been involved with 6 or more commercial releases (as performer, player, producer, engineer, etc.), join NARAS (Grammy Association) and become a voting member and let your voice be heard. Go to www.grammy.com

8) Enter your songs in contests and submit your recordings for awards. Let others hear your music. And, if you win, toot your horn!

9) Get a website. Get involved with Social Media. Get your music on the internet through on-line distributors like Amazon.com, CD Baby, OySongs (Jewish), Pandora, etc. Sign up for digital distribution.

10) Believe in yourself. Don't just dream it, do it!

WHO ARE YOU?

Performing IS a business. You may want to just sing or tell stories or do comedy, but somebody has to make things happen for you. Somebody has to get the word out about you, somebody has to handle your bookings, somebody has to take care of your travel and touring arrangements, somebody has to publish your compositions or writings, somebody has to do your accounting, etc. For many of us – we ARE "somebody". And we have to be many "somebodies". We not only create original material, but we have to be publicist, booking agent, manager, accountant, travel agent, costumer, blogger, etc. all rolled into one.

Decide who you are and what audience(s) you want to reach
To begin, answer the following questions:
- What do you do well?
- What do you do that is unique?
- Are your skills good enough to be a performer?
- In what type of setting are you most comfortable performing?

- Do you perform best on your own or in a group?
- Do you want to travel?
- What type of audience enjoys what you do?
- What type of audience do you enjoy performing for?

Some people are great songwriters, but not great performers. Some people are best suited for performing in small groups and small venues. And some people just come to life when they are performing in a huge hall or at a big outdoor festival. What appeals to you? Where are you most comfortable? Know your strengths and capitalize on them and know your limitations and ask for help.

Some people do one type of thing and they do it very well. You may be a comedian or an opera singer, or a camp song leader. Find what you do best and cultivate it and market it. You are not in competition with anyone else. Everyone has something unique to offer. So don't feel like you have to be better than someone else. You just have to be YOU and see if you have what it takes to offer a unique performance that will be enjoyed by an audience. You have to be the best YOU can be!

Create an image around who you are, always being true to yourself. Be comfortable in your own skin. Be confident that you can share your talents. Study, practice, network and learn from those who have information to give you.

It is also very important to create a business plan. Do a short term (3-5 years) and a long term (5-10 years) plan. Set goals for yourself. What would you like to be doing in 5/10 years? What would you like to have accomplished professionally in 5/10 years? How will you grow your business? How will you grow yourself? How will you keep up with ever changing technology? How will you manage everything? It does not have to be elaborate. But, definitely write out some short and long range goals for yourself.

"You always need to have somewhere to go in order to grow."

HOW DO I LET PEOPLE KNOW ABOUT ME?

Once you have determined who you are and what audience you want to reach, go out and find that audience. You may have to do some research or network with others. Attend conferences and meetings that you think might suit what you do. Join organizations that can put you together with others who do what you do or what you want to do. Join listservs. Get a web site. Join social media outlets like Facebook and My Space. Post videos on YouTube. Talk to other people whom you admire. Gather contacts, search out mailing lists, participate in showcases. Network, network, network. Learn, learn, learn.

Create information about yourself to give to others. Get some business cards. Design stationery, a brochure. Make a demo DVD. All of these things should reflect your unique image and your personality. You may want to consider creating a logo that identifies you and what you do. A graphic designer can help you create a logo and some of these items. You want everything you give out about yourself to follow a "theme". (This is called "branding"). If you have a logo, it should be on everything you give out to people. You should include your name and your contact information on everything you give out to people about you or your business. And a photo of you does not hurt either. People want to feel a connection to you. A friendly photo immediately gives them a visual of who you are.

Another way to "build a buzz" is by getting reviews in music magazines, newspapers, or blogs . Get as many reviews as you can. Check your local clubs and bookstores for these kinds of magazines and submit your material for review. Also try to hit local entertainment papers, or papers with local entertainment sections. Invite them to review a live performance. If they like you, maybe they'll review your stuff. Do your homework! Go to your local library or browse the internet for magazines, newspapers and radio stations that review and play independent label recordings. Use the resources provided in this manual. Music is a business and you have to do lots of research to get ahead and stay ahead.

CREATING A PRESS KIT

A press kit is essential if you want to get the word out about what you do as a performer. Many people have press kits on their websites, where interested people can download information about them and get photos. But, there will be times where you may still need a "paper" press kit. A press kit should reflect your personality and your unique image. A good press kit should be readable, concise and clear. Otherwise, people will not take the time to read it. It should always be accompanied by a cover letter on your stationery. The press kit should be put in a two-pocket folder that has a cut out for your business card. You should have something eye catching on the cover of the folder - a good color photo or collage of photos of you in action. A good press kit (digital or paper) should contain:

1) **Cover letter**: This letter is addressed to a particular person and quickly tells who you are and what you want. Make sure the cover letter contains all of your contact information.

2) **Biography/Professional Highlights:** This is a resume. The bio should be no more than one page and should chronicle the history of your work and achievements as a performer. I like to use a bulleted list instead of paragraphs. It is easier on the eyes.

3) **Photo**: Spend the money to get professional photos taken. Ideally, take photos in both black and white and color. You may have occasion to use both. You can post these on your website. Have a quantity of 8 x 10 B/W glossies made and always print your name and contact information somewhere on the photos. These photos can also be used for autographs after a show.

4) **Press clippings/Reviews**: Include articles that have been written about you and your performance or songwriting. You may want to create a one-page collage of various articles or reviews.

5) **Quote sheet**: A quote sheet is a collection of flattering remarks that have been said about you and your music. Keep it to one page and always list who said the quote and their position.

6) **Touring list/venue list**: If you have performed a lot, you may want to include a tour schedule or a list of venues where you have performed. This helps to show that you are actively touring and shows your track record. You may also want to include a list of references from places where you have recently performed.

7) **Business card**: Always include a business card in a press kit. Usually folders will have a die-cut area where the card will fit.

8) **Demo/Work Sample:** If at all possible include an audio or video demo with the press kit. It is often helpful to know something about the listening preferences of the people who will receive the press kit. Some people like to listen to music in their cars. Others will prefer an mp3 upload. More and more people are asking for video samples instead of audio. Finding out ahead of time what format your prospect prefers can be the difference in whether or not your demo gets seen/heard. Always put your name, phone number and website on the demo.

9) **Descriptions of Programs You Offer:** A brief description of the programs you can offer a client – concerts, residencies, master classes, etc.

10) **Technical Rider:** a description of your technical needs if hired (or you can wait until hired to send this out)

Again, remember to put your name and contact information on every piece of anything that is in your press kit. If something gets pulled out of the kit, there will always be a way for someone to know whose information it is and how to get in touch with you.

Because I do lots of performances for families, I will often do fun things with my press kits like include stickers or toys or confetti in the packaging. I usually send it in a colorful envelope instead of white/beige. Do something to make your press kit stand out and be remembered, but make sure it still reflects your unique image.

DEVELOPING A WEBSITE

A website is absolutely essential in this day and age if you want to let people know about you and what you do. There are websites such as Register.com, GoDaddy and Word Press which allow you to create your own website using their templates. But, if you really want to have a website with a unique image that gives you the freedom to do just about anything you want, I recommend hiring someone who does this for a living. There are many people who can design a web site for you and I would highly recommend looking to the expertise of others unless you have these skills yourself. The most important thing in choosing a web designer is to make sure they are listening to what you want. Check out other sites they have designed. Do all the sites look alike or does each site reflect a unique personality? Can you get along with the person? Can you afford the person? Who will maintain the site? It does not matter where your web designer/master lives. Everything can be done via the internet and they are only a phone call or Skype away. Two web designers that have experience designing websites for performers that I can personally recommend are:

Matt Cohen – It Won't Byte - http://www.iwbyte.com/
Rick Lupert - Rick@PoetrySuperHighway.com

I strongly suggest getting and registering a domain name that easily identifies who you are. Try to see if your name or your performance name is available. Your web designer can help you register your domain. They can also help you handle hosting services for your site. An easy do-it-yourself website host/design company is **Register.com** (www.register.com). They offer a variety of templates for you to be able to create and maintain your own website. However, you are limited to the templates and designs they offer. This is an affordable way to get yourself on the web, but it may not provide you with the flexibility you are looking for.

A basic web site should contain:

    a. A home page
    b. About the artist or bio page
    c. How to contact the artist page
    d. What you offer (types of concerts, programs, residencies, etc.)
    e. Items for sale (if applicable)

You may also want to include:
    a. Reviews, news clippings, recommendations/quotes page
    b. links to other sites that you enjoy or support
    c. lyrics to your songs
    d. activities or contests
    e. your touring history
    f. current performance/travel schedule
    g. a press kit
    h. samples of your work – audio/video
    i. guestbook
    j. blog

A web site is a great place to sell your products. Through **Pay Pal (www.paypal.com)** you can set up a way for customers to purchase your products with credit cards. Since I added this feature to my web site, my sales have doubled.

MARKETING OPTIONS

Other than your press kit and a web site, there are lots of other creative ways to market yourself to the world at large. First, it helps to have people to send marketing materials to. Develop a fan base. Every time someone purchases one of your products, add their name and information to your database. When you perform somewhere, have a mailing list that people can sign and add these names to your database. There are a variety of programs that you can use for keeping a database on your computer (Excel, Access, etc.) There are several methods I use to keep in touch with clients and fans:

Postcards - sending postcards to a fan base is an inexpensive and effective way of keeping in touch with people. Two great sources for ordering bulk post cards are **Vistaprint (www.vistaprint.com)** and **Modern Postcard (www.modernpostcard.com)**. You can easily design your cards on line or pay a little more for custom cards. It is cheaper than mailing a letter and it is a great way to advertise yourself or a new product. Often, I use postcards instead of a smaller business card to give to people to advertise what I offer. I also enclose a post card with every order I send out to a customer. I usually sign the back with a note of thanks.

E-mail/Blogs - create a monthly e-mail newsletter/blog or send e-mails to targeted groups of fans at various times of year. Use social networking (**Facebook**, **My Space**, etc.) If you know you are traveling to a particular part of the country, you can target fans living in that part of the country to let them know that you will be in town and send information about your concerts. This is also a way to keep fans informed of new products, awards, etc. NuMuBu is a social network just for musicians. Check them out at **www.numubu.com**.

Download Cards – These are business card size cards that have a special code on them. You can either sell them or give them away. They allow someone to go to a website where your music is available for sale and download either a song or two or even an entire album. These are a great marketing tool. I ordered mine from CDbaby.

Street Team – send flyers and information out to fans who live in cities where you will be performing. Ask these fans to put up flyers and get the word out about your event. In exchange you can offer them a free ticket to your show or a CD.

Always check with local television and radio stations and newspapers to see if they will do a story on you. Anytime you win an award, release a CD, do a major performance…this is newsworthy. Let people know and get your face out there.

MAKING A CD

The truth about making CDs is that just about anyone can make one in these technology filled times. You can spend a little money (a few thousand) or you can spend a lot ($10,000+) for a quality product that will produce sales in stores. Recently, actual CD sales have decreased as more and more people are downloading music to digital players, computers and tablets. Very few people under the age of 30 are purchasing CDs. I, personally, like having the whole CD package. I like reading the liner notes and seeing the lyrics. I like seeing the pictures of the performers. But this is a generational thing. Most of our children will probably never purchase a CD. All of their music will be downloaded.

I primarily sell CDs after a show. If people like what you do, they want to take a piece of it home with them. But, CD sales have taken a back seat to downloads. So, instead of ordering 1000+ CDs at a time, I am now ordering 200 or less at a time.

There are some things to consider before you create a CD. First, ask yourself the following questions:
- Why am I making a CD?
- Is it for you and your friends/family/community?

- Would you like to make it available in the broader marketplace?
- Do you have national exposure or just a local following?
- Are you selling your songs or your musical talents?

I will tell you that if you are not actively performing it is difficult to sell CDs. If you are not planning to tour or if you do not think this is where your strengths lie, then really think about where you will have avenues to sell your CD. Just because you are writing songs, does not mean the next step is to put these songs on a CD. Every songwriter is not a performer. Some can study and work to get themselves to a place where they do a respectable job and they feel comfortable. But others are more suited to writing and trying to find others to perform their works. This is a decision only you can make. And it is a process. It all takes time.

There are also options today to just download individual songs without the need to produce an entire CD. You can produce songs one at a time and make them available for download. You can also transcribe your songs and make the sheet music available for sale. Places like **Cdbaby**, the **Orchard**, **OySongs** (for Jewish music), etc. can help you do this.

My advice would be that if you do not intend to perform actively, do not spend a lot of money on the CD. Go to a good studio and make a nice clean copy with instruments you play or you can easily hire a few others to play. There is no need to fully orchestrate this stuff. But make it sound pleasant with some basic instruments -- guitar, bass, drums, keyboard. (I have heard a number of recordings with just voice and guitar or voice and piano that are lovely). You may not even want to sing the tunes yourself. You may want to hire people to do the vocals. If your main motivation is to get the songs out there, make them sound as good as you can. Then, it will be the songs you are "selling" not your ability to perform them.

I will give you a great example of this. I have a friend who writes wonderful songs that teach basic Hebrew (she is Israeli and she teaches in a day school). She does not perform herself, but she uses music in the classroom and she writes great songs. She produced a CD and songbook of her songs. She hired a vocalist with a very pleasant voice to sing them and she hired musicians to play the songs very simply. She markets the product for the value the songs provide. And it is selling nicely.

If you feel that you want to actively "go on the road" and perform, then you will need a great product to sell. People will hear you and if they enjoy it, they will want to buy a copy of what they have heard. In this scenario, you will need to have a good, quality product. And it is with this scenario that I would spend more money to produce a CD.

A quality CD does take probably a minimum of $10,000 to produce. I have financed all of my CDs myself. My first one I did in 1981 and saved for several years to be able to afford it -- of course things were cheaper then too. I have never put another dime into my business. I made my second recording based on sales from the first, and so on. I just released my 12th recording. If you have a product that sells well, it will pay for itself and allow you to make subsequent products. If you have to keep putting money into the creation of products, maybe you need to rethink your business plan. You do have to spend money to make money, but there comes a point where you must ask yourself, is this profitable?

That said, there are also some creative ways to find funding to produce a CD:

1) Find some sponsors (kind of like "sugar daddies") who believe in what you are doing and are willing to float you a no-interest loan to do the project. As you make money, you pay them back. So it is an investment of sorts. You give them credit on the CD, etc.

2) There is also a website called **Kickstarter** (https://www.kickstarter.com/start) where you can post your creative project on the internet and solicit people to help fund it. You have to raise the money in a specified

amount of time and you provide various levels of "perks" to those who donate.

3) I also have friends who have produced CDs in memory of someone and the loved ones family has offered the money to cover CD costs as a memorial to their loved one.

4) Many state arts councils will give grants to individual artists toward making recordings especially if they have some sort of archival or historical value.

Once you have the money together, it is time to decide how and where you are going to record your songs.

RECORDING & PRODUCING YOUR CD

If you have the money to invest in a project, go for it. Go to a good studio with a knowledgeable engineer. Be prepared BEFORE you go into the studio so that you can do the project efficiently. In the studio, time is money. Most studios charge by the hour, so the less time you spend in there, the better off you are from a financial standpoint. You do not, however, want to sacrifice quality. If you want to record the project in your own home studio, make sure that you have quality equipment and the knowledge to do the job well.

Most of us are considered "independent" artists or "indie" artists. We do not have a big record deal. There is no record company spending large amounts of money to produce our CD and get it out to the public. Therefore, you are your own producer. (There are a number of engineers who own studios who can also act as a producer for you. They can be another set of ears and make suggestions for arrangements, instrumentation, etc.) Once you are out of the studio, you are on your own. It is up to you to sell your product. As an independent music producer, you must be prepared to do lots of work and never give up trying to get your product out there. You have made a major investment of time, talent and money — so let others know about it. Again, do your homework. Research distributors, venues for performing, radio stations, press reviews, etc. When you produce and "plug" your own product, you will be totally behind it. Often a major label will push your product for a while and then find the next best thing. If you have a good product you can push it indefinitely.

SELLING & MARKETING YOUR RECORDING

Anyone can go into a recording studio and make a CD. The big question is what are you going to do with it? Is your music a hobby or a business? If your music is a hobby then you are probably content to give copies away to all of your friends and relatives. But, if you are serious about your music, you want people to buy your CD. The only way people are going to buy your music is if they hear your music. You have to make people aware of your music and you have to create the demand for your music. You must perform. You must try to get distribution and airplay and you must take the BUSINESS of music seriously.

Most radio markets in the U.S. have some radio station that will play local (home grown) music. In addition, college radio stations are a great way to get your stuff on the air. In your local market, go to the stations and visit with the program director (PD). Talk with the music director (MD). Get to know the DJs or show hosts. And don't just do it in your local area. Contact radio stations in other markets as well. It is always a good idea to contact local radio stations in a city prior to playing a gig there. They may be willing to interview you while you are in town or give you some advance publicity. Also, check out satellite radio opportunities. There are stations playing very specific genres in this market. Check to see if you fit in to any of them and send them your music. Always follow-up. Be persistent.

Go to local stores and see if they will take your CDs on consignment. This means that they don't pay you unless people buy your CD. Most local record stores will do this for you, especially if you are getting radio play and they can make some money by selling your product. Some local stores may even let you perform in them. If you are able to leave your CDs with a store on consignment, make sure you have an invoice indicating how many copies you are leaving, for how long and what the wholesale and retail prices are. Leave one copy with the store and keep one copy for yourself. Keep all of these invoices in an alphabetical file or on your computer. Check in with these stores every few months to see how sales are going and if they need more product. Also, make sure you are paid for what they sell. It is on you to keep up with this.

Larger record stores may be less likely to have room for your stuff, unless you are the hottest thing in town. Check them anyway. You may be able to find an exception to the rule. The worst that can happen is that your stuff isn't placed in their stores. The best that can happen is that people buy your stuff. The more people buy, the more you can sell to the store the next time. Try to visit with the store's staff. Maybe you can get someone to play your music over the store's sound system and people may like what they hear and want to buy the CD. Do some research on distributors who carry your type of music. Get to know them and see if they will purchase some of your music on a trial basis to put into stores. If you are playing in a city out of your local area, call ahead to see if record stores there will sell your stuff. Make sure they know about your gig there. Offer to do a brief in store concert in exchange for a chance to sell your recordings.

Internet distribution is a must for anyone who has a CD today. Amazon.com (**www.amazon.com/advantage**) will sell your products through their Advantage program. I also highly recommend Cdbaby (**www.cdbaby.com**). This is an internet presence devoted to the Independent Musician. They will sell your CDs and give you $10 for each one sold. They will also sign you up to distribute your music digitally. They will keep track of all of your digital downloads, you can track your sales and they will send you money each month. They also produce download cards and will license your music for synch rights. Check them out!

There are also several free internet music sites like Jango Radio and Pandora (www.jango.com and www.pandora.com). You can sign up to have them play your music. You pay a small fee based on the number of times they play your music. They have tools for you to build a fan base and check statistics on who listened to your music, where they are from and how they happened upon your stuff.

For specifically Jewish music, check out www.**Oysongs.com**. They exclusively distribute independent Jewish music...both audio downloads and sheet music.

UPC/ISBN BAR CODING FOR PRODUCTS

UPC (Universal Product Code) and **ISBN (International Standard Book Numbering)** are ways for retailers to identify each of your individual products. If you are going to seriously market your recordings to major retail stores, you will need to apply for a UPC code. If your music is to be sold in the bookstore market, you will need what is called an ISBN number and bar code as well. Because of the vast variety of products out there, this is a standard way of cataloging and identifying products. Most major retail outlets use scanning equipment and you will be required to have UPC and/or ISBN coding on your product before they will work with you. Some CD/book manufacturers will provide you with these codes as part of the package you pay for. However, for the serious musician who will probably release multiple products, it is probably a good idea to get your own numbers and get a quantity of them for future products.

To find official information on UPC coding, contact info@gs1us.org or (937) 435-3870 or go to **www.gs1us.org**
You can request information on ISBN coding from **International Standard Book Numbering**, (www.isbn.org or call 888 269-5372). Both of these will cost you some money, but it was worth it to me to have my own codes. You will be sent information on how to figure your UPC codes for each product and you will be sent a list of ISBN numbers assigned to you. You must request how many ISBN numbers you want. They are assigned to you in a

sequence. You must now have 13 digit ISBN numbers. They are currently charging $250 for 1-10 numbers with an annual renewal fee of $50.

After you receive your codes, you will need to add them to your products. You can have your CDs printed with this information on them or, if you already have a back stock of CD inserts printed without codes, you can have stickers made for them. UPC generally includes a list of manufacturers who will print UPC/ISBN stickers for you in the materials they send you.

Many CD manufacturers provide bar codes as part of their packaging. If you don't want to bother with getting your own, ask the manufacturer if they will provide one for you. If you go with one from the manufacturer, it will not be uniquely yours. It will be tracked back to the CD manufacturer. If you are selling thousands of recordings and having things tracked through Soundscan, I would recommend investing in your own bar codes.

Soundscan is the official method of tracking sales of music and music video products throughout the United States and Canada. Anyone selling a music product with a unique UPC bar code can register with Soundscan. Registration is free. Go to: http://titlereg.soundscan.com/soundscantitlereg/

COPYRIGHT INFORMATION

Under the current Copyright Act, the author of a song (the work) has a valid copyright in the song from the moment the song is "created." By "created", the Act means that the song is either written down or recorded in such a way that someone can hear or see it. Creation can be recording the song on your computer or other device, such as a tape or CD. Creation can be writing out the music. Creation is NOT humming the song. There must be something physical on which the work is embodied.

Copyright protection is acquired automatically when a work is "created". The definition of "created" is when a work is fixed in a copy or recording for the first time. A song is considered "published" when copies of the song have been distributed to the public by sale OR by other transfer of ownership, and/or by rental, lease, or lending. As soon as you write your song down on paper or record it on tape, you have a copyright. But there are several reasons why you should officially register it for the greatest amount of protection. First, registering with the Copyright Office gets you a piece of paper that tells the world that you own the copyright in your song. Second, you can't even THINK of suing someone for copyright infringement without having first registered with the Copyright Office. Third, there are certain damages that you can only obtain for violations that occur AFTER your copyright is registered with the Copyright Office. As long as you have "intent to register" the copyright, you may display the copyright symbol on your recording.

Your copyright should be protected by the Copyright Act, and not by the "Poor Man's Copyright" (Poor Man's Copyright is what people refer to when they put their song or recording in an envelope and mail it to themselves. When they receive the package, they don't open the envelope. This provides proof that the individual or group created the song at LEAST as early as the postmark on the envelope. Therefore, if someone claims that they, in fact, are the owners of the song, the original Artist can present the UNOPENED envelope as evidence that they created the song at an earlier time.)

The first thing you need to do is request the proper forms from the Copyright Office form request line. The phone number is (202) 707-5959 or (877) 476-0778 toll free. You can write to them requesting forms at **US Copyright Office**, Library of Congress, 101 Independence Ave., SE, Washington D.C. 20559. It usually takes about two weeks to receive your forms. The easiest way to get forms is to go to the Copyright Office web page at **http://www.copyright.gov/**. You can download and fill out the forms right there.

You need to know which forms to request. No matter what forms you need, you should also request a copy of "Circular 1 Copyright Basics" or read this on their website. This is a very concise and easy to understand booklet of basic information on copyrights. Read it first before filling out any forms because it answers a lot of questions. If you want to register only your lyrics or only instrumental music, request "Circular 50 Copyright Registration for Musical Compositions." If you want to register a song with lyrics and music embodied on a tape or CD, request "Circular 56 Copyright for Sound Recordings" (Form SR). Both Circular 50 and Circular 56 come with details about registering music and include the appropriate forms. You may download these circulars at their Web Site. **http://www.copyright.gov/circs/**

When you make a recording, you have two separate copyrights (excluding any cover artwork which can also be copyrighted separately). First, you have a copyright in the music and lyrics of the song (or the song itself). If the songs were transcribed to sheet music, that would be the first copyright. The second copyright is the copyright in the sound recording (the actual recording of the song). If you re-record the song at a later date, you would not have a new copyright in the underlying song, but you would have a new copyright in the sound recording.

When registering an audio recording, you want to register both the underlying music and lyrics (if you are the composer) and the sound recording. Circular 56, and specifically Form SR within Circular 56, is what you will want to fill out. Form SR allows you to register both the lyrics and music and the sound recording in one copyright, and perhaps more importantly, with one fee.

Another question is whether to register each individual song as a separate copyright or register the recording as a whole. Registering a recording with one copyright registers all the songs on that recording for <u>one fee</u>. The only advantage to registering each individual song is that each song has its own entry in the Copyright Office register. This could be advantageous if someone wanted to find out who owned the copyright to a song but did not know what audio recording it came from. They could search for the song and find an entry. But, who wants to pay $35 or more for each song? You can also submit sheet music as a "collection" for one copyright fee instead of copyrighting each song separately.

If you have original artwork for the cover of your tape of CD, you may consider copyrighting that as well. Request "Circular 40 Copyright Registration for Works of the Visual Arts". In this Circular, you will find Form VA that is nearly identical to the forms for registering music.

You may not obtain copyright for a song title. But be aware that using the exact title of a song that has established itself as part of the culture, can open the doors for a lawsuit based on property rights in the title, which belong to the copyright owner of the famous song. The sound recording copyright (registered with form SR) is for the protection of the sounds on the recording, and usually belongs to the record company who has released the recording. The PA copyright form is the copyright of the song on the CD, and usually belongs to the publisher of the song. If the same person owns the recording and the song (as most independent musicians do), only one SR form is needed.

Please note, that the copyright office currently charges $35 for electronic filing and $65 for paper filing. So, do try to do everything online....it will save you money.

You should put a copyright notice on all published copies of the song or recording. A circle with a small 'c' [©] in it is the usual mark, but the word 'copyright' is also acceptable. Follow the mark with the year and the songwriter's name. Note: the year stated is the year the song was 'first published', not when the song was written. Unpublished works need no copyright notice, but it is still a good idea to put the mark and use the phrase, for example "unpublished 1995, James Jones". A copyrighted work has protection under the law for the life of the songwriter, plus 70 additional years after his/her death.

PERFORMANCE RIGHTS AND MECHANICAL RIGHTS

The performance rights and the mechanical rights to a song are the two separate rights granted to the owner of the song. **Performance rights** are granted in order for the song to be sung or played (recorded or live), in a public place or on radio and television. It is the function of a Performance Rights Organization to grant these licenses and pay the owner of the song for the use of the song on the radio, TV, hotels, clubs, colleges, restaurants, elevators, doctor's offices, stores, etc. There are three Performance Rights Organizations in the United States. They are **BMI** – www.bmi.com (212) 586-2000, **ASCAP** – www.ascap.com; 800 95-ASCAP (212) 621-6000 and **SESAC** – www.sesac.com (headquartered in Nashville with other regional locations) 615-320-0055. After copyrighting, you may want to affiliate with one of these music licensing companies. BMI, ASCAP and SESAC offer licensing services which track club, radio and TV play to ensure that you are paid performance royalties when others perform or play your song.

Mechanical rights are given in order to reproduce the song on actual CD's, and to sell the reproduced copies to the public. It is the responsibility of record labels or individual record producers to pay mechanical royalties to the owner of the song, for the sale of CD's. Once a song has been released on a recording, anyone else has the right to record it <u>if they pay the required mechanical rights for the use of the song</u>.

Most mechanical rights requests are handled by the **Harry Fox Agency** – www.harryfox.com (212) 834-0100. As of 2014, the mechanical royalty rate (or statutory rate) for physical recordings and permanent digital downloads is 9.10 cents (.091) per copy per song for the first five minutes of the musical composition and 1.75 cents for every minute after that for each copy distributed. Adjustments to this rate are made every two years. Perhaps the easiest way to keep up with this is, if you use a song someone else wrote, send them a check for the royalty rate multiplied by the number of copies of the CD you produce (If you use a song written by Shlomo Mashuga, and you order 1000 Cds, you should send Shlomo a check for $91 (.091 x 1000 copies) for the use of his song. It is much easier to send a check each time you order than to keep up with numbers of sales. Harry Fox also provides information on rates for interactive streams, limited downloads and ringtones. The current statutory mechanical royalty rate for ringtones is 24¢ per copy. Check the Harry Fox website for more detailed information.

When working with colleagues whose songs you wish to record, I suggest contacting them directly. They will let you know what they require.....some will accept the current statutory rate; others may ask that a donation be made to a charity; and still others may allow you to record their song with no strings attached. But remember, the ethical and legal thing to do is pay the composer for the use of their song.

PERFORMING

Most of us are in this business because we want to perform and share our music with others. This is an important part of the business. You may want to start locally. Look for venues that hire local musicians to perform. Audition for opportunities. Offer your services to sing at weddings, parties, etc. Look for festival and showcase opportunities to get exposure. Look for ways to diversify what you have to offer. Where does your music fit? What venues offer opportunities to perform your type of music? Look at all possibilities.

Determine a pay scale for what you want to be paid? Will you charge less locally than you do to travel? Will you charge by the hour or by the performance? Will you charge more for one type/style of performance than you do another? Do some research on what others in your area are being paid to do similar work. What can the market bear? Be fair to everyone....people talk and compare. Be fair to yourself too. Your talent is worth something. Don't give it away for free or for too little. There are always opportunities to do something for free for a good cause, but you should be paid most of the time. After all, this is your business!

Develop a contract for when you are hired. Never do anything on a handshake. You need to protect yourself and those who are hiring you. A contract – even a very simple one – insures this. At the very least, a contract should contain the following:

Who is hiring you? (get a contact name, address, phone and email)

What are they hiring you to do?

Where are you doing it? When (date and time) are you doing it?

What are they paying you? In addition to your fee, are they responsible for any travel costs? Meals? Accommodations? Ground Transportation? Mileage?

Do you require a deposit upon signing the contract? When is payment due in full? Who should they make the check payable to?

Outline your technical needs. Outline any other personal needs (non-smoking room, whether or not you will accept home hospitality, must have bottled water, etc.)

Are you able to sell your products after the performance? Will you give them (or do they require) a percentage of sales?

Always include a cancellation clause. What happens if they cancel? What happens if you cancel? You may want to look at samples of other contracts to see what should be included here.

The contract should be signed and dated by you and the venue hiring you. Always keep a copy.

There are so many details to take care of when you tour. I won't rewrite the book here, but I will refer you to check out the many wonderful books on the resource list. And, remember, I am available for consulting if you need guidance.

Also, don't forget Performer Etiquette. Here are a few tips:

So that there are no misunderstandings, make sure that you have spelled out all of your requirements, both technical and personal, in the contract.

Make sure that you have a name and phone number of a contact person and someone at the venue (put it in your phone so it is handy)

Arrive early

Stick to your agreed upon performance time. Do not run overtime.

Try to mingle with fans after the performance.

Be sure to thank those who hired you (and the tech people) during the show. It is always nice to thank those who hired you after the show as well in the form of an email, handwritten note, etc. once you get back home.

You might want to ask the person who hired you to write a "review" or recommendation that you can use to secure future gigs. If they liked the performance, their recommendation can go a long way in the eyes of one of their colleagues.

TIPS FOR MANAGING YOURSELF

Treat your music like a business and keep good records

Prepare a career plan and set short and long term goals

Outline specific tasks and strategies for reaching your goals

Once you reach a goal — set the next one

Stay focused on your plan

Keep your resume up to date

Find a way to accept credit cards for sales – check out Square (www.squareup.com) Pay Pal also has a device (www.paypal.com)

Get feedback and constructive criticism from friends, family and colleagues

Do your homework. Continuously read books and articles on the music business

Take advantage of opportunities to advertise/promote your music

Participate in a few showcases periodically just for the exposure

Get access to the internet. Set up an e-mail account and a webpage

Join musicians' organizations

Attend music conferences and seminars

Network

Use Social Networking to get the word out.

Don't let success go to your head. Be thankful and move on.

Get away occasionally and seek inspiration from unlikely places and sources

Keep your financial records in order (keep receipts)

Keep your mailing list (fan list) up to date

Find outlets to practice your craft. See what works and what does not.

Be creative

Keep some good press or nice notes around to look at when you have a bad day

Know who your friends are and don't forget them

Believe in yourself and don't give up

DIVERSIFY:
THINKING OUTSIDE OF THE MUSIC BOX

I am living proof that you can make a living as a musician even if you do not live in a big city with lots of music resources. But you have to be creative and you have to be willing to diversify. In other words, you have to look beyond just performing in your comfort zone and see what other doors might be open for you to make money (or get exposure) making music.

Some things to explore might be:

Teaching music

Running a summer music camp

If you perform for children, libraries and schools can be a nice source of work

Work on your songwriting skills and enter some songwriting contests

Work part time at a music store (the discounts are nice and you meet lots of people looking for musicians)

Talk to your Visitor and Convention Bureau about possible opportunities they might have for musicians. They probably get calls from groups coming into town for conventions or meetings who are looking for entertainment

Check with local churches or synagogues to see if they need an organist, pianist, song leader, choir director, band member, etc.

Check with local schools or universities to see if they are looking for teachers, musicians for special events or mentoring

Make sure your local Arts Council knows about you. They can often refer business your way and may even know of some grants that might be available to you

Join any local music organizations so you can meet and network with other musicians

Offer workshops on some aspect of music that you have expertise in that you feel others might want to learn (sound engineering, using Finale or other music software, music of a particular culture, how to use social media, etc.)

Volunteer to sing occasionally at a senior center or a hospital that has an Arts in Medicine program

Offer to perform on a program for a local service organization like Rotary, Lions Club, Garden Club, etc.

TAX TIPS FOR MUSICIANS

You may download forms from the IRS, at www.irs.gov/Forms-&-Pubs. If your music is your business, then you need to treat it like a business especially for tax purposes. Here are some helpful tips:

Get a business license

Keep good books and accurate records

Consider incorporating your business (consult an attorney)

Get a post office box for business mail

Open a separate checking account for your business

Print business cards

Copyright your songs and register your original songs with a performing rights organization

Save clippings or ads about your music/performances

Consider setting aside a room/space in your home for an office

Keep mileage records of travel for your music business, save receipts from business trips

To deduct business expenses, fill out Schedule C and file it with your Federal Form 1040. If you are self-employed, you will have to also file Schedule SE (you must pay self-employment taxes if your net earnings from self-employment were over $400). If your business is a corporation, you will need to file Form 1120.

In IRS publication 535, it says, "To be deductible, a business expense must be both ordinary and necessary. An ordinary expense is one that is common and accepted in your trade or business. A necessary expense is one that is helpful and appropriate for your trade or business." What follows is a list of some categories of items for which you may be able to claim deductions:

Instruments

Equipment & Accessories (cases, microphones, amps, etc.)

Consumable supplies (strings, picks)

Music books, directories, manuals

Sheet music and audio music

Subscriptions to trade magazines

Promotional items (CDs, demos, photos, posters, press materials)

Office supplies (paper, stamps, envelopes, etc.)

Fees related to maintaining your web site and e-mail access

Rent for storage, equipment, office or practice space

Membership in professional organizations

Advertising

Professional fees (attorneys, managers, accountant)

Copyright and other registration fees

Lessons & Instructional Seminars

Travel expenses

Home office deduction — The rules on this have recently changed and are more favorable to the self-employed

To avoid tax problems, document everything. Here are some suggestions for items you should keep copies of in a tax file:

Accurate records of all business activities

Press releases

Gig Flyers, postcards, posters

Your mailing list

Press clippings and ads

Receipts and invoices for everything you purchased or earned that is business related

All correspondence

A calendar which accurately reflects all gigs and business related details

When in doubt, ask a professional. If it is questionable, don't deduct it. Keep all of your tax-related records for at least seven years.

Useful IRS publications:

Publication 334 - Tax guide for small businesses

Publication 946 - How to depreciate property

Publication 583 - Starting a business and keeping records

Publication 587 - Business use of your home

Publication 911 - Tax information for direct sellers

Section 179 of the tax code deals with expenses and deductions for capital assets (instruments, equipment, etc.)

For more info: **www.irs.gov**

RESOURCES

Join as many **Organizations** and **Associations** as possible that relate to your area of performance and become aware of sources for funding and grants. Note: As of the publication date of this book, all resources were accurate.

ACUM, (Israel's mechanical rights association), www.acum.org.il/
A & R Registry, music business contacts, legal & publishing info; www.aandronline.com
AFMindie.org, www.afmindie.org; articles and resources to help independent musicians, Affiliated with American Federation of Musicians
Allure Media Entertainment, www.allureinc.com, lots of great resources
American Conference of Cantors (ACC), professional organization of Reform Cantors, www.accantors.org
American Federation of Musicians (AFM), Paramount Building, 1501 Broadway, Suite 600, New York, NY 10036, (212) 869-1330; www.afm.org
American Songwriter Magazine, 121 17th Avenue South, Nashville, TN 37203, (615) 244-6065, www.americansongwriter.com
Americans for the Arts, helpful books; www.artsusa.org
ArtistsFirstMusic.com, Music supervision services, Encino, CA, 323 325-2000
ASCAP, (212) 621-6000, info@ascap.com, www.ascap.com
Association of Independent Music Publishers (AIMP), www.aimp.org
Association for Independent Music (AFIM) Formerly known as NAIRD. Dedicated to promoting the independent recording industry. www.a2im.org
Billboard Magazine, (subscriptions and information), www.billboard.com
BMI, (mechanical rights organization); various offices around the world, www.bmi.com
Cantors Assembly, Professional association of Conservative Cantors, www.cantors.org

Cdbaby, great resources for independent musicians, lots of free resources, CD & digital sales, etc., www.cdbaby.com, **highly recommended**
Children's Music Network, www.cmnonline.org
Country Music Association (CMA), Nashville, TN www.cmaworld.com
Creative Musicians Coalition, Great place for independent musicians producing their own material. Peoria, IL, aimcmc@aol.com; www.creativemusicianscoalition.com
Foundation Center, publishes many sources for finding grants, library@fdncenter.org; www.foundationcenter.org
Fractured Atlas, New York, offers lots of resources for musicians and artists including insurance, and info on specially priced studio space in major cities; www.fracturedatlas.org; (888) 692-7878
Getty Center for Education in the Arts, Los Angeles, CA, (310) 440-7300; www.getty.edu
Gospel Music Association (GMA), Nashville, TN, (615) 242-0303; www.gospelmusic.org
GrantsWeb, grant related info on the internet including grants databases, activities and funding opportunities, www.srainternational.org
GTM (Guild of Temple Musicians), affiliate of ACC, www.thegtm.org
Harry Fox Agency, Inc. / National Music Publishers' Association, 601 W. 26th St., Suite 500, New York, NY 10017, (212) 834-0100; www.nmpa.org/hfa.html handles mechanical and synchronization licensing for copyrighted musical compositions, and the distribution of royalties based on those licenses.
Hitquarters, music industry search directory, www.hitquarters.com
IndieGuide, www.indieguide.com; complete DIY musicians resources, free e-books, **highly recommended**
Internet Resources for Non-Profit Organizations, produced by University of Wisconsin - Madison, lists info about grants and funding, (608) 262-6431, http://grants.library.wisc.edu

Judy Caplan Ginsburgh, PO Box 12692, Alexandria, LA 71315, (318) 442-8863, www.judymusic.com, judy@judymusic.com; available for speaking, training and consulting

Kennedy Center Alliance for Arts Education Network, Kennedy Center for the Performing Arts, Washington, DC (202) 467-4600, (800) 444-1324, www.kennedy-center,org/education/kcaaen

Musician Magazine's Guide to Touring & Promotion, www.musiciansmag.com

Nashville Songwriters Association International (NSAI), (800) 321-6008, www.nashvillesongwriters.com

National Endowment for the Arts, 1100 Pennsylvania Ave., NW, Washington, DC 20506, (202) 682-5400, www.nea.gov

Record Label Resource, resources for indie musicians, www.recordlabelresource.com

SESAC - Performing Rights Organization, Nashville, TN & other locations throughout the world, (615) 320-0055, www.sesac.com

SOCAN - Canadian Performing Rights Organization (Society of Composers, Authors & Music Publishers), www.socan.ca

Songquarters, Affiliated with Hitquarters, submit songs to artists and publishers, www.songquarters.com

Songwriters Network, www.songwritersnet.com

TAXI, connects artists and songwriters with major record labels, www.taxi.com

Women Cantors Network, www.womencantors.net

Women in Music National Network (WIMNN), www.womeninmusic.com

Women in the Arts, Inc., Madison, WI, host a national women's music festival, http://wiaonline.org

Read **Books** and **Trade Magazines** & watch **Videos** about making a living in the arts and touring. **Note:** You may find some of these titles at your public library. You should be able to order most of these books from your local bookstore. Believe it or not, I actually own most of these books...collected over 30+ years in the business. And almost all of these books have received 4 or 5 star reviews from readers.

An * after a title means that all of these books can be ordered from Amazon.com, Most are also available in Kindle edition. (www.amazon.com)
A # after a title means that all of these books can be ordered from Musicbooks Plus, an on-line bookstore specializing in Music books. Their web address is ---- (www.vaxxine.com/mbp/)

All Area Access: Personal Management for Unsigned Musicians, Marc Davison, 384 pages, 1997 *
All You Need to Know About the Music Business, Donald S. Passman, 480 pages, 7th edition 2009 *
Anything You Want: 40 Lessons for a New Kind of Entrepreneur, Derek Sivers (founder of CD baby), 77 prolific pages!, 2011 *
Art of Record Production, Richard Burgess, 228 pages, 1998 *
Billboard Magazine, www.billboard.com
Billboard Guide to Music Publicity, James Pettigrew, Jr., 176 pages, 1997 *
Book Your Own Tour : The Independent Musician's Guide to Cost-Effective Touring and Promotion, Liz Garo, 181 pages, 1995 *
Arts, Culture & the Humanities Grants Guide, Foundation Center, NY, 1992
Breaking into the Music Business, Alan H. Siegel, 352 pages, 1991/revised for 21st century * #
Business Forms & Contracts (In Plain English) for Crafts People, Leonard D. DuBoff, 110 pages, 1993, includes CD Rom *
Complete Guide to Getting A Grant, L. Blum, 368 pages, 1996 *

Dance Music Programming Secrets, Roger J. Brown, 450 pages, 1996 *

Doing Music and Nothing Else, Peter Knickles, educational seminar, call 800-448-3621

Don't Just Applaud, Send Money, Alvin H. Reiss, Theater Communications Group, 200 pages, 1995 *

Foundation Grants to Individuals, Foundation Center, NY, 1995

From Idea to Funded Project: Grant Proposals for the Digital Age, Julia Jacobsen, 176 pages, 2007 *

Get It in Writing: The Musician's Guide to the Music Business, Brian McPherson, 352 pages, 1999 *

Getting Business to Come to You, Paul & Sarah Edwards, 704 pages, 1998 *

Getting Radio Airplay :The Guide to Getting Your Music Played on College, Public and Commerical Radio, Gary Hustwit, 128 pages, 1998 *

Getting Your Sh*t Together: A Manual for Independent Artists, www.gyst-ink.com

Going Pro: Developing A Professional Career in the Music Industry, Kenny Kerner, 208 pages, 1999 *

Great Ad! Low Cost Do-it Yourself Advertising, Carol Wilkie Wallace, 352 pages, 1990 *

Guide To Getting Arts Grants, Ellen Liberatori, 272 pgs, 2006 *

Homemade Money: Bringing in the Bucks, Barbara Brabec, 320 pages, 2003 *

How to Be a Working Musician : A Practical Guide to Earning Money in the Music Business, Mike Levine, 282 pages, 1997 *

How to Be Your Own Booking Agent and Save Thousands of Dollars, Jeri Goldstein, 492 pages, 2000 * **highly recommended!!**

How to Have Your Hit Song Published, Jay Warner, 402 pages, 2006 *

How to Make and Sell Your Own Recording, Diane Rappaport, 258 pages, 1999 * #

How to Make Money : Scoring Soundtracks and Jingles, Jeffrey P. Fisher, 780 pages, 1997 *

How to Make Money Performing in the Public Schools, David Heflick, 82 pages, 1993 *

How to Make More in Music, James Gibson, 107 pages, 1984 *

How to Pitch and Promote Your Songs, Fred Koller, 208 pages, 2001 *
How to Succeed in the Music Business, Alex Batterbee, 208 pages, 2008 *
If You've Got A Dream, I've Got A Plan, Kelley Lovelace, 160 pages, 2003 *
Legal Handbook for Small Business, Marc Lane, 250 pages, 1989 * or American Management Association, Amacom books, ISBN 978-0814459515
Making a Living in Your Local Music Market, Dick Weissman, 272 pages, 4th edition, 2010, **highly recommended** *
Making It in the Music Business : A Business and Legal Guide for Songwriters and Performers, Lee Wilson, 256 pages, 3rd edition, 2004 *
Making Music Make Money: An Insider's Guide to Becoming Your Own Music Publisher, Eric Beall, 272 pgs., 2003 *
Making Music Your Business : A Guide for Young Musicians, David Ellefson, 148 pages, 1997 *
Money for Performing Artists, Suzanne Niemeyer, 268 pages, 1991 *
The Musicians Atlas, now only online, updated annually, www.musiciansatlas.com
The Musicians Guide to Touring and Promotion, may be out of print, published by Billboard, 2006, (212) 536-5208
Music Business Handbook & Career Guide, David Baskerville, 640 pages, 1995 *
Music Law: How to Run Your Band's Business, Richard Stim, 421 pages, 2009 *
Music, Money, and Success: The Insider's Guide to Making Money in the Music Business, Jeffrey & Todd Brabec, 512 pages, 6th edition 2008 * #
Music Publishing: A Songwriters Guide, Randy Poe, 152 pages, 3rd edition, 2005 * #
Music Publishing:The Real Road to Music Business Success, Tim Whitsett, 260 pages, 6th edition, 2009 *
National Directory of Record Labels and Music Publishers, Barbara Taylor, 1996 * #
National Guide to Funding in Arts & Culture, Foundation Center, NY, 1992

National Standards for Arts Education, Consortium of National Arts Educ. Assoc., Music Educators Nat'l Conference, 1994, ISBN 1-56545-036-1

Networking in the Music Business, Dan Kimpel, 151 pgs., 2000*

Networking in the Music Industry: How to Open the Doors to Success in the Music Business, Jim Clevo & Eric Olsen, 240 pages, 1993 *

101 Ways to Make Money Right Now in the Music Business, Bob Baker, Rockpress Publishing, 1992 #

Permission Marketing: Turning Strangers Into Friends and Friends into Customers, Seth Godin, 256 pages, 1999*

Personal Budget Planner: A Guide for Financial Success, Eric P. Gelb, 1992 *

Presenting Performances, Thomas Wolf, ACA Books, 189 pages, 6th edition, 1991 *

Purple Cow: Transform Your Business By Being Remarkable, Seth Godin, 224 pages, new edition, 2009 *

Recording Industry Sourcebook, Barry Cleveland, 376 pages, 11th edition, 1999 *

Releasing an Independent Record: How to Successfully Start and Run Your Own Record Label in the 1990s, Gary Hustwit, 175 pages, 6th edition, 1998 *

Shortcuts to Hit Songwriting: 126 Proven Techniques for Writing Songs That Sell, Robin Frederick, 290 pages, 2008 *

Six Steps to Songwriting Success, Jason Blume, 304 pages, 2nd edition, 2008 *

Songwriting: The Words, the Music and the Money, Dick Weissman, 152 pages, 2001 *

Songwriter's Market, 2010 edition, Writer's Digest Books, 432 pages, 1996 *

Songwriters Market Guide to Song & Demo Submission Formats, Donna Collingwood, 153 pages, 1994 *

Star Tracks : Principles for Success in the Music & Entertainment Business, Larry E. Wacholtz, 284 pages, 1997 *

Successful Grantwriting Tips: The Manual, B.A. Browning, Grantsline, 1991 (out of print)

Successful Lyric Writing, Sheila Davis, 1990 * #

The Artist's Resource Handbook, Daniel Grant, 248 pgs., 1997 *
The Bottom Line is Money: A Comprehensive Guide to Songwriting and the Nashville Music Industry, Jennifer E. Pierce, 1994 *
The Check is Not in the Mail: How to Get Paid More in Full, on Time, at Less Cost and Without Losing Valued Customers, Leonard Sklar, 299 pages, 1991 *
The Chord Wheel: The Ultimate Tool for All Muscians, Jim Fleser, 12 pages, 2000 *
The Complete Handbook of Songwriting, Mark & Kathy Liggett, 352 pages, 1993 *
The Complete Idiot's Guide to Music Theory, Michael Miller, 336 pages, 2nd edition, 2005 *
The Copyright Handbook: What Every Writer Needs to Know, Stephen Fishman, J.D., 528 pages, 10th edition, 2008 *
The Craft and Business of Songwriting, John Braheny, 400 pages, 3rd edition, 2007 *
The Craft of Lyric Writing, Sheila Davis, 350 pages, 1984 *
The Future of Music: Manifesto for the Digital Music Revolution, Kusak, 197 pages, 2005 *
The Future of the Music Business: Music Pro Guides, Steve Gordon, 362 pages, 2008 *
The Home-Based Entrepreneur: The Complete Guide to Working At Home, Linday Pinson and Jerry Jinnett, 170 pages, 1993 *
The Indie Band Survival Guide, Randy Chertkow & Jason Freehan, 352 pages, 2008 * (may be downloadable for free at www.indieguide.com)
The Inner Game of Tennis, W. Timothy Gallwey, 1997, ISBN: 9780679778318 *
The Law (In Plain English) for Crafts People, Leonard D. DuBoff, 148 pages, 1993 *
The Music Business: Career Opportunities and Self-Defense, Dick Weissman, 416 pages, 3rd edition, 2003 *
The Music Business Explained in Plain English: What Every Artist and Songwriter Should Know to Avoid Getting Ripped Off, David Naggar, 160 pages, 3rd edition, 2010 *
The Music Business Contract Library, published by Hal Leonard, 320 pages, 2008 *

The Musician's Business & Legal Guide, Mark Halloran, 448 pages, 4th edition, 2007 *
The Musician's Guide to Making & Selling Your Own CDs & Cassettes, Jana Stanfield, 170 pages, 1997 *
The Musician's Guide to Reading & Writing Music, Dave Stewart, 120 pages, 2nd edition, 1999 *
The Musician's Guide to the Internet, Gary Hustwit, 88 pages, 2nd edition, 2002 *
The Musician's Internet: Online Strategies for Success in the Music Industry, Peter Spellman, 176 pages, 2001 *
The Nashville Music Machine: The Unwritten Rules of the Country Music Business, Dan Daley, 288 pages, 1997 *
The New Rules of Marketing & PR: How to Use Social Media, Online Video, Mobile Application, Blogs, News Releases, and Viral Marketing to Reach Buyers Directly, David Meerman Scott, 288 pages, 2010 *
The Professional Musician's Internet Guide, Ron Simpson, 198 pages (includes CD), 2001 *
The Professional Singers Handbook: The Complete Guide to Becoming a Successful Singer, Gloria Rusch, 216 pages, 1998 *
The Publicity Handbook, David Yale, 464 pages, 2nd edition, 2001 *
The Publicity Kit, Jeanette Smith, 352 pages, 1995 *
The Real Deal : How to Get Signed to a Record Label from A to Z, Daylle Deanna Schwartz, 288 pages, 2002 *
The Road Show: A Handbook for Successful Booking and Touring in the Performing Arts, Rena Shagan, 267 pages, 1985 *
The Savvy Musician: Building A Career, Earning a Living and Making a Difference, David Cutler, 350 pages, 2009, highly recommended *
The Self Promoting Musician, Peter Spellman, 264 pages, 2000 *
The Songwriters Handbook, Tom T, Hall, 164 pages, 2001 *
This Business of Artist Management , Xavier M., Jr. Frascogna, H. Lee Hetherington, 304 pages, 2nd edition, 2004 *

This Business of Music and **More About This Business of Music**, Sidney Shemel & M. William Krasilovsky, 576 pages, 10th edition, 2007, **highly recommended** *
Tim Sweeney, publishes downloadable books and resources for musicians, www.tsamusic.com
Touring Without Tears, Marcia Lane, 1995 (pamphlet)
Working For Yourself: A Guide to Success for People Who Work Outside the 9 to 5 World, Phillip Namanworth & Gene Busnar, 312 pages, 1985 *
You Can Make Money in Music : Everything a Musician Needs to Know to Become Steadily Employed As a Live Performer, Craig Warren Colley, 1995 *

The internet is an amazing place to do research. There are thousands of places to visit to learn about the industry. There is even room for you to create your own "home page", blogs, participate in social media, etc. to let others know about you and your talents! Below are a few web sites that should be useful.

Amazon Books - www.amazon.com (Order books about music); Sell your music www.amazon.com/advantage
ASCAP - www.ascap.com (performing rights org)
AFIM - Association for Independent Music, www.afim.org
AMISG - (American Music Information Source Guide)
Billboard - www.billboard.com
Bluesman Newsletter - not really a blues site; has great resources for music teachers and a music graphics library www.jumpoint.com/bluesman/newsletter.html
BMI - http://bmi.com (performing rights organization)
CDBaby – great place to sell your music, www.cdbaby.com (owned by DiscMakers)
CMC - Creative Musicians Coalition   www.aimcmc.com
CMW - Children's Music Web   www.cmnonline.org/
Copyright Office - http://lcweb.loc.gov/copyright/
Discmakers - www.discmakers.com (publish many helpful booklets for musicians)
Get Your Sh*t Together, www.gyst-ink.com, great website with lots of business info for artists

Indie Guide – www.indieguide.com, great resources for musicians
Jango Radio – www.jango.com
Lil' Hank's Music Site - www.halsguide.com/ (Lots of useful info for songwriters and musicians)
MTV News - www.mtv.com
Music Books Plus - www.musicbooksplus.com (Great site for ordering books about music)
Musician's Friend Catalog - www.musiciansfriend.com
National Music Publisher's Association (Harry Fox Agency) - www.nmpa.org; (info. on obtaining mechanical rights to record music of others)
NuMuBu – www.numubu.com (free music industry social business network)
Offbeat/La. Music Directory - www.offbeat.com
Orchard – www.theorchard.com - distributes music downloads for indie artists
OySongs – www.oysongs.com - especially for Jewish Indie Musicians
Patent and Trademark Office - www.uspto.gov/ (Info. on obtaining patents and trademarks)
Song Lyrics - www.azlyrics.com; www.songlyrics.com; www.lyrics.com
Tara Publications - www.jewishmusic.com (resource for Jewish music)
TAXI - www.Taxi.com - (helps songwriters plug their songs)
Transcontinental Music/Soundswrite – resource for Jewish music including music for choirs, www.transcontinentalmusic.com,
Zebra Music - www.zebramusic.com (jam packed with resources for musicians)

For many more sites, read The Musicians' Guide to the Internet by Gary Hustwit

Some fun resources:

All Music Gifts – www.allmusicgifts.com
The **Music Stand** catalogue - catalogue of hundreds of music related items - t-shirts, pencils, music boxes, awards, accessories, etc. www.themusicstand.com
Friendship House catalogue - catalogue of music awards, gifts and teaching aids, contains lots of books. www.friendshiphouse.com
Dowling Music – for all your sheet music needs and lots of musical accessories and gift items. www.dowlingmusic.com

ABOUT THE AUTHOR

Judy Caplan Ginsburgh is available for consulting work and work for hire. She has over 30 years in the music business as a performer, songwriter, manager, event planner, presenter and consultant. Below are some highlights from Judy's career:

- Vocal Performance degree from Indiana University Jacobs School of Music

- Recording artist with 14 recordings, 3 books and 1 DVD to credit; professional singer specializing in Early Childhood Music and Jewish music; presenter of interactive and educational musical concerts and residencies for family audiences.

- **Jubilation Foundation Fellowship** – Tides Foundation – 2011 & 2012
  Arts Awareness & Education Award - Arts Council of Central Louisiana – 2010
  National Art Education Association Award for Best Work Outside the Profession - NY, 2007
  Artist Entrepreneur Grant from the Louisiana Division of the Arts - 2006
  Runway Award from American Red Cross for Best Model Program - 2006
  Blair Sadler International Healing Arts Award for innovative use of arts - Chicago, 2006
  LA Governor's Arts Award: Performing Artist of the Year - 1999
  Religious Heritage of America Music Award for outstanding contributions to the field of Jewish music - Pennsylvania, 1990

- Nationally recognized speaker/educator on the subject of children's music, discipline & transitions, and integrating music into curriculum. Speaker's Bureau of the Association for

Childhood Education International; Trainer for SDE (Staff Development for Educators); Certified Louisiana Pathways Trainer; frequent speaker at NAEYC; CAJE; RIF; Headstart; regional and state educational conferences

- **Louisiana Roster Artist** since 1988; La. Touring Directory Artist; **Southern Arts Federation Juried Touring Artist**; Featured La. Artist at Southern Arts Federation Conference; Panelist, La. State Arts Conference - 1997; Recipient of 2 Artist Mini Grants

- **iParenting Media Award** - 2007 & 2004
  Children's Music Web Awards: Best Compilation for Preschoolers & Best Religious Recording for Preschoolers - 2003
  Just Plain Folks International Song Contest - 3rd place, **Children's Song**, 2002
  Pegasus Award - Best Inspirational TV Show, Dr. Kastl's Psychology Show - 2000
  #1 best-selling Jewish Children's Recording on the Web - 1998 - present
  Children's Music Web Finalist - 1999; 2002
  National Parenting Center Seal of Approval - 1997
  Parents' Choice Foundation Silver Honor - 1998 & 1994
  Parents' Choice Foundation Seal of Approval - 1992
  Mazel Tov Award - Best Jewish Children's Recording - Houston, 1989

- Named one of the **Top Ten Jewish Children's Performers** and one of the **Top Ten Jewish Female Vocalists in the world** by Moment Magazine & Tara Publications
  Named one of the **Top Ten Jewish Children's Performers** and one of the **Top Ten Jewish Female Vocalists in the world** by Moment Magazine & Tara Publications

- **Project Director/Author/Performer** for the URJ (Transcontinental Music) early childhood music curriculum, **My Jewish World** - 2003; Original songs featured on URJ projects: Complete Jewish Songbook for Children; Project Manginot; Torah Alive; Shalom Israel; Good Morning, Good Night; Shabbat Shalom; CHAI Curriculum; The Complete Chanukah Songbook; Songs For A Jewish Head Start; Featured on Compilations: Remembering Robin; Chanukah Feast (Hungry for Music); Original song featured on Countdown with Keith Olbermann – 2008

- **Arts Education Coordinator** for the Arts Council of Central Louisiana - 2004-2006
  Founder & Executive Director of **Central Louisiana Arts & Healthcare, Inc.** - bringing innovative arts into healthcare settings - 2003 - present
  Founder & Director – Jewish Entertainment Resources - (marketing and educating Jewish performers; producing multi-media shows nationally); 1994-2007
  Southern Region Director for Guitars in the Classroom; 2004 – present

www.ingramcontent.com/pod-product-compliance
Lightning Source LLC
Chambersburg PA
CBHW071801040426
42446CB00012B/2653